MAGA

Make the Alphabet Great Again

By Connie S. Tution

ISBN: 979-8-3481-6041-8

To Donald J. Trump and his supporters. I hope you enjoy.

A is for Administration.

Donald Trump has some exciting picks for his administration! His Secretary of the Treasury is a trust fund manager, his Secretary of Defense has never served, and his head of the Department of Health and safety doesn't believe in vaccines.

B is for Bankruptcy

Donald Trump has filed for bankruptcy four times! That's a lot!

C is for concept.

Donald Trump has a concept of a plan to fix healthcare.

D is for diapers.

Donald Trump wears adult diapers for the times that he can't make it to the potty in time.

E is for eating.

Donald Trump accused immigrants in Ohio of eating dogs and cats.

F is for felony.

Donald Trump has 34 felonies.
That's a lot!

G is for Gaetz.

Trump picked Matt Gaetz to be Attorney General. Unfortunately, Matt couldn't do this job, because he was accused of doing naughty things with young girls.

H is for Heritage Foundation.

The Heritage Foundation wrote
Project 2025. Donald Trump says
he has nothing to do with the
Heritage Foundation.

20
Mandate for Leadership
The Conservative Promise
25
Foreword by Kevin Roberts, PhD
Edited by Paul Dans and Steven Groves

I is for insurrection.

On January 6. 2020, many people stormed the capital building because they were mad that Donald Trump wasn't going to be President that time.

J is for Jesus.

Many of Trump's supporters compare him to Jesus, writing worship songs and calling him the "chosen one."

K is for Klan.

Donald Trump once referred to some members of the Ku Klux Klan is "very fine people."

L is for losers.

On the other hand, Donald Trump once referred to some Prisoners of War as "losers."

M is for McDonald's.

Donald Trump likes McDonald's very much. He even "worked" at one for a day!

N is for Nationalism.

Nationalism is the belief that your country is the very best and is above reproach!

O is for orange.

Donald Trump's makeup is very orange.

P is for Putin.

Vladimir Putin is the head of Russia. Trump always has nice things to say about his good friend Putin.

Q is for queer.

Donald Trump does not like the LGBTQIA+ community because he does not feel like they embrace traditional values.

R is for refugees.

Donald Trump plans to build a wall and also deport thousands and thousands of refugees.

S is for Stormy.

Donald Trump has a special friend named Stormy Daniels who he paid a lot of money to not tell people about their friendship. Unfortunately, it wasn't his money!

T is for tariffs.

Trump plans to implement very big tariffs, which the people or companies purchasing products from other countries will have to pay.

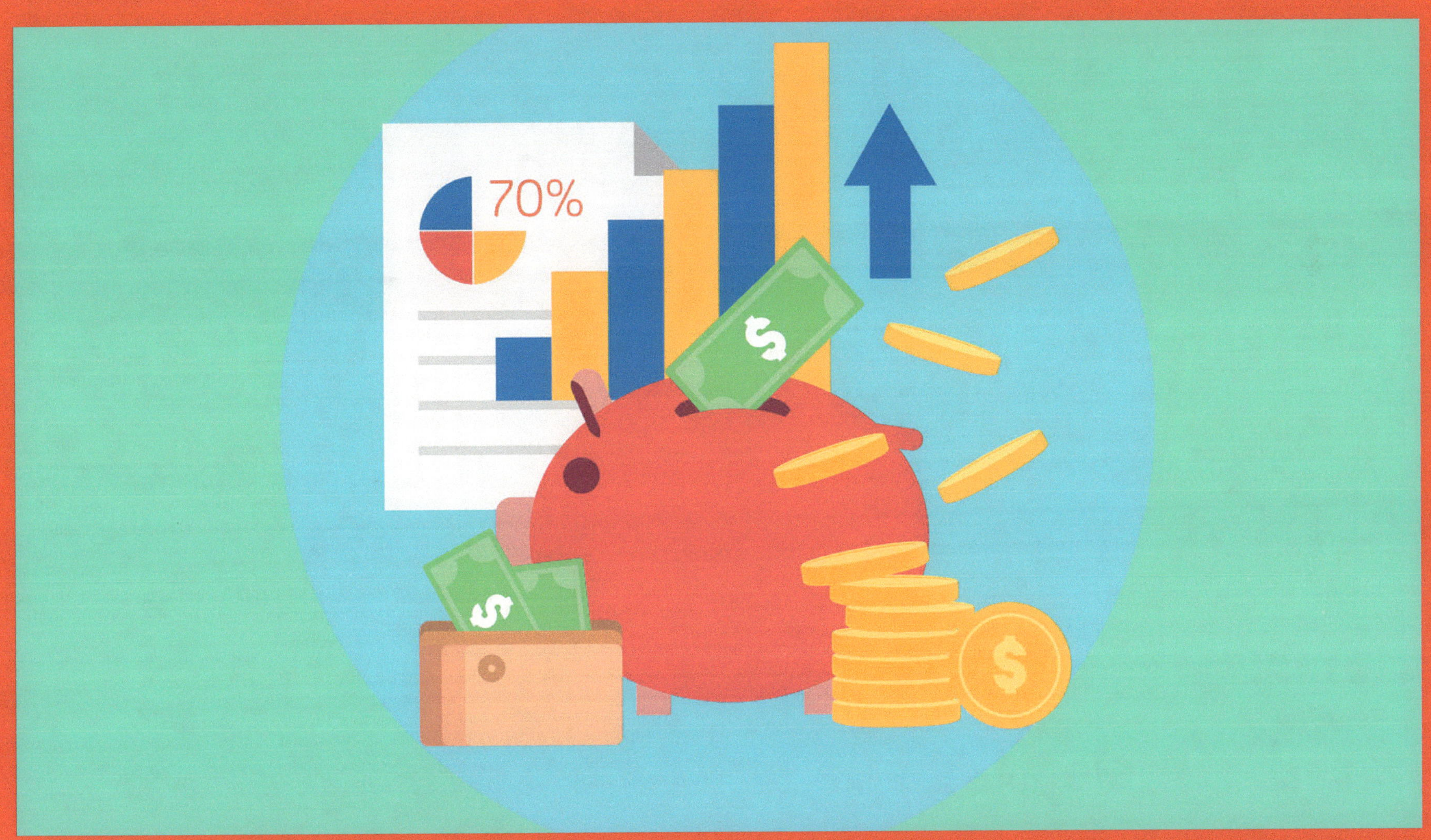
70%
$

U is for Ukraine.

Trump believes that he can bring peace to Ukraine very easily. It might mean they have to give up some land, but he thinks that's a fair price to pay.

V is for vasectomy.

Vasectomies would be an excellent way to avoid unplanned pregnancies. However, we aren't allowed to tell boys what to do with their bodies. That's not nice!

W is for women.

Trump says that he loves women and will protect them whether they want it or not!

X is for Twitter.

Donald Trump's good friend Elon Musk owns Twitter. Trump likes to tweet very, very much.

Y is for yellow journalism.

Yellow journalism is journalism that is sensationalized and not always true, especially to matters of politics or war.

Z is for Zionism.

Zionism is the belief in the divine right of Israeli people. That means they can kill all the people in a whole country if someone hurts them.